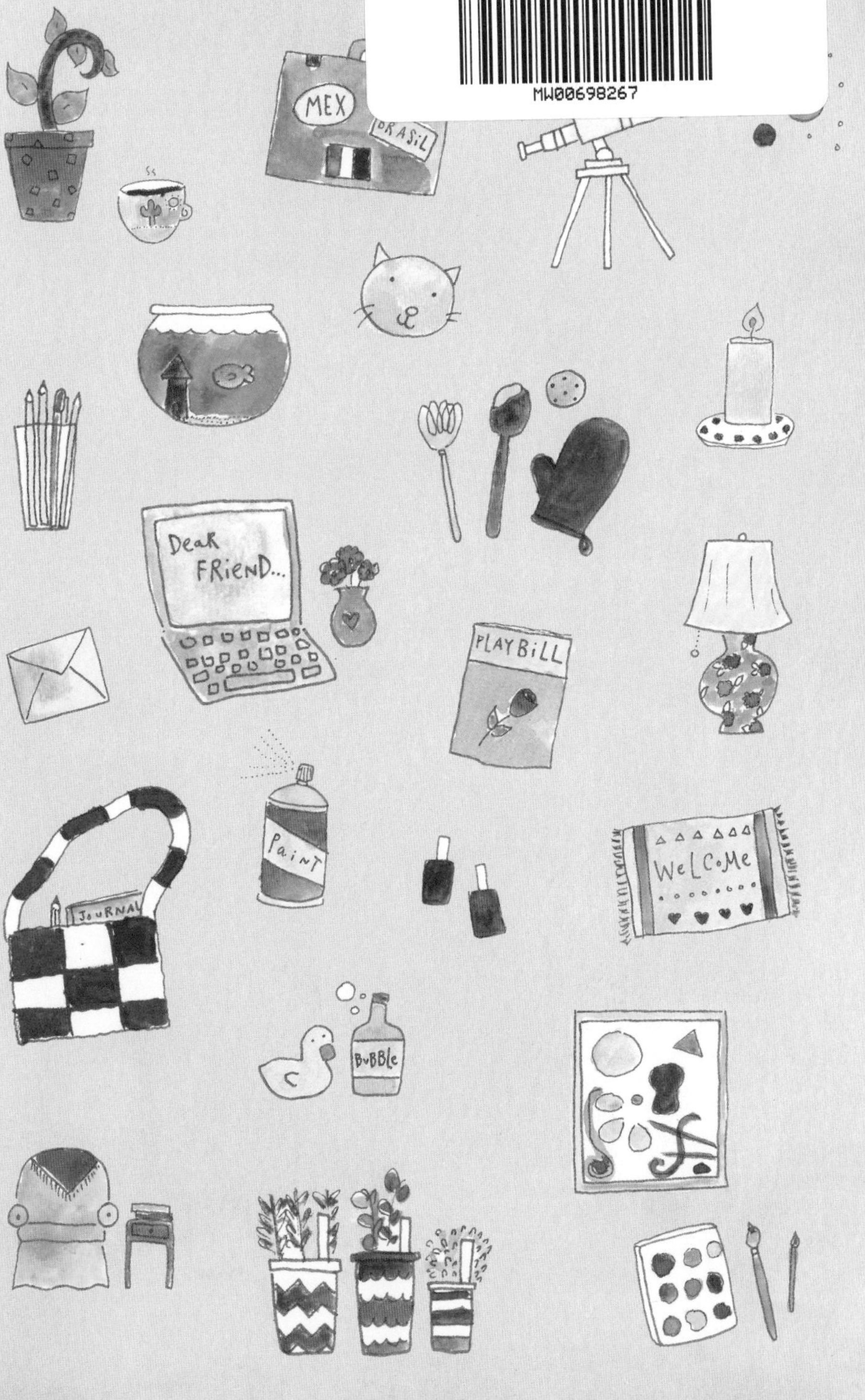
MEX
BRASIL
Dear FRIEND...
PLAYBILL
Paint
WELCOME
JOURNAL
BUBBLE

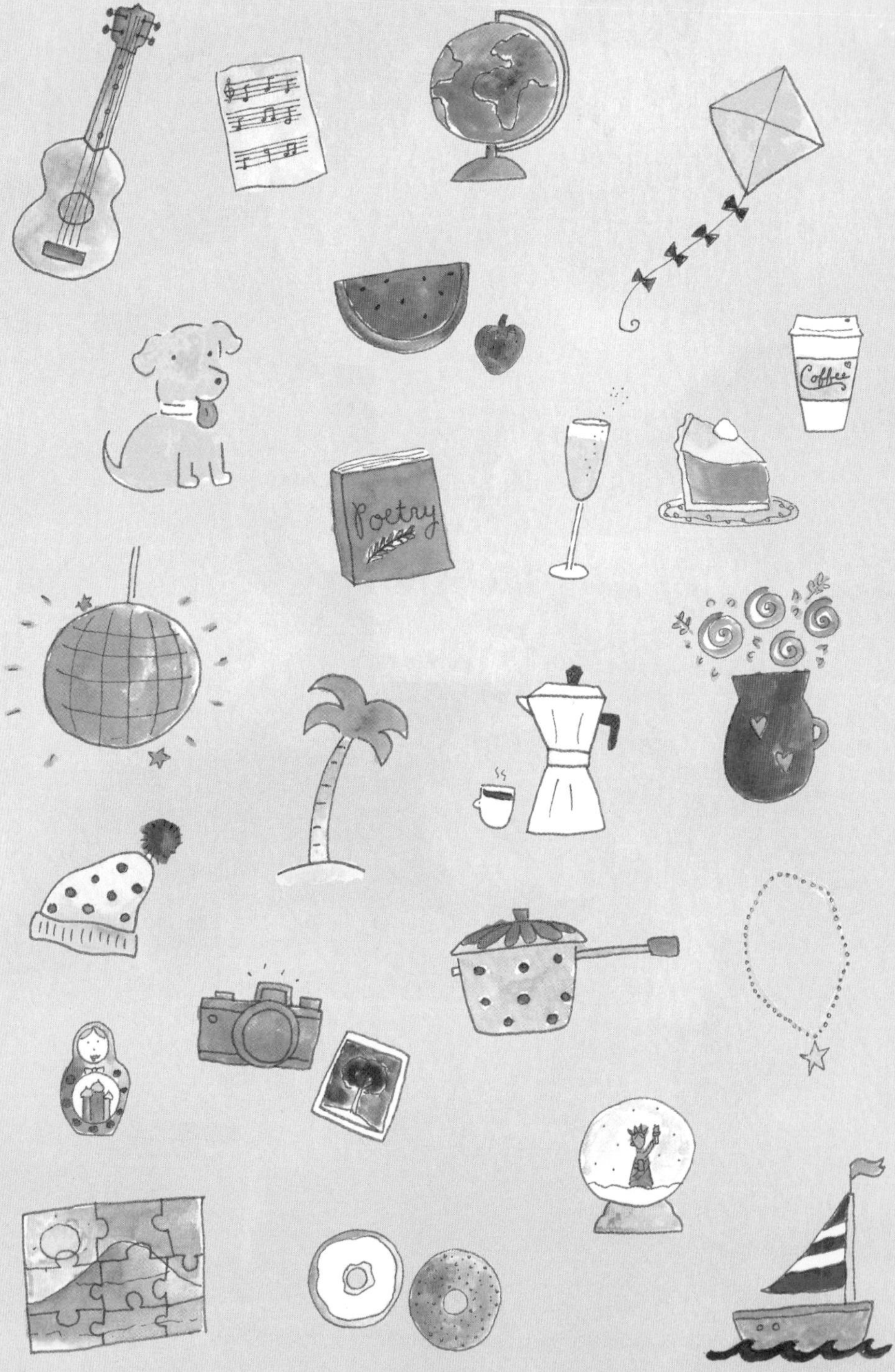
Coffee
Poetry

FROM THE DESK OF:

Contact info (address & phone):

GROW, BLOOM, FLOURISH

A 52-Week PLANNeR FoR SeLF-ReFLecTioN

MaRi ANDRew

CLARKSON POTTER/PUBLISHERS

NEW YORK

clarksonpotter.com

CLARKSON POTTER is a trademark and POTTER with colophon
is a registered trademark of Penguin Random House LLC.

ISBN 978-0-593-13961-5

Printed in China

Design by Jessie Kaye
Cover illustrations by Mari Andrew

10 9 8 7 6 5 4 3 2 1

First Edition

INTRODUCTION

I've always been a planner. Every time I sit down to think about my intentions and hopes for a new week, month, or year, I find clarity I didn't know I needed—goals I haven't articulated, accomplishments I haven't yet celebrated. While I'm planning, I find that there are friends I'd like to see more of and activities I want to do more often. I also see things I'd like to do less of! So long as I go into my planning sessions with a nonjudgmental perspective, I find I can learn a lot about myself. It's like giving my heart and mind a checkup.

In this planner, I've added some tools that I find useful during my checkups, and I encourage you to personalize them as much as you want!

1. MONTHLY CHECK-INS AND WEEKLY AFFIRMATIONS:
   Once a month, take a beat and get honest with yourself about what's going well and what parts of your life could use a bit more attention and love. You can use this data to write your weekly affirmations, which can be as simple as "I am grateful" to something more elaborate, depending on your goals.

2. HABIT TRACKER:
   Setting the habit of creating art every day is how I taught myself to be an illustrator! Habit-setting shouldn't be boring; you can get in the habit of doing the things you really love that you may not naturally set time for. You might want to add in wellness, money-saving, or mindfulness habits, too. But please don't feel like you have to set a certain number of habits and don't beat yourself up if you're not meeting your goals. That might be good data that you're just not as interested in something as you thought you were—that's fine! On to the next!

3. SELF-COMPASSION:
   I'm not sure about you, but sometimes when I set goals or make resolutions, I feel self-conscious—they're not lofty enough, too ambitious, not realistic, or far too practical. Be gentle with yourself! You're allowed to find joy in anything you want; your goals are for your own happiness. Whenever I accomplish my goals, it's because I set authentic intentions that feel totally life-giving to me . . . even if they don't make sense to other people.

Remind yourself often: This is your planner and this is your life! Enjoy!

xo, MaRi

MY INTENTIONS

Consider your priorities, goals, and whims for the year ahead.
What do you want most for yourself? Dream big!

What do you hope to know about yourself this year?

_____

_____

_____

What are your favorite things about yourself right now?

_____

_____

_____

Which word or phrase will guide you this year?

_____

_____

_____

How do you want to expand your community this year?

_____

_____

_____

How do you want to feel in your body this year?

_____

_____

_____

What do you need to feel supported this year?

_____

_____

_____

What do you want to learn by the end of the year?

_____

_____

_____

What are some steps you can take toward your wildest dreams this year?

_____

_____

_____

MY VALUES

What is most important to you in each of these realms of your life?
And don't forget: values can change over time!

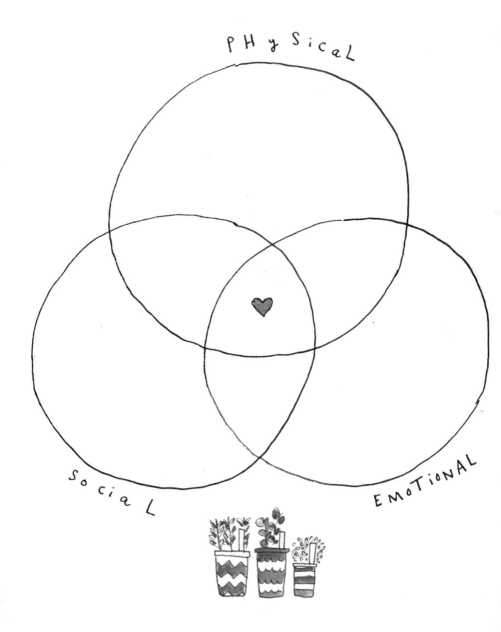

MY VISION BOARD

Paste in scraps of paper, magazine clippings, or photos that exemplify
how you want to live your life this year. Add to it as the year progresses!

YEAR 1

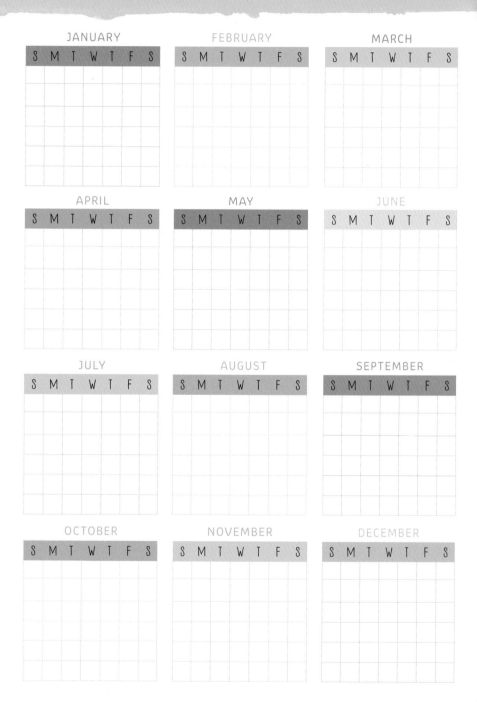

JANUARY

S	M	T	W	T	F	S

FEBRUARY

S	M	T	W	T	F	S

MARCH

S	M	T	W	T	F	S

APRIL

S	M	T	W	T	F	S

MAY

S	M	T	W	T	F	S

JUNE

S	M	T	W	T	F	S

JULY

S	M	T	W	T	F	S

AUGUST

S	M	T	W	T	F	S

SEPTEMBER

S	M	T	W	T	F	S

OCTOBER

S	M	T	W	T	F	S

NOVEMBER

S	M	T	W	T	F	S

DECEMBER

S	M	T	W	T	F	S

YEAR 2

JANUARY						
S	M	T	W	T	F	S

FEBRUARY						
S	M	T	W	T	F	S

MARCH						
S	M	T	W	T	F	S

APRIL						
S	M	T	W	T	F	S

MAY						
S	M	T	W	T	F	S

JUNE						
S	M	T	W	T	F	S

JULY						
S	M	T	W	T	F	S

AUGUST						
S	M	T	W	T	F	S

SEPTEMBER						
S	M	T	W	T	F	S

OCTOBER						
S	M	T	W	T	F	S

NOVEMBER						
S	M	T	W	T	F	S

DECEMBER						
S	M	T	W	T	F	S

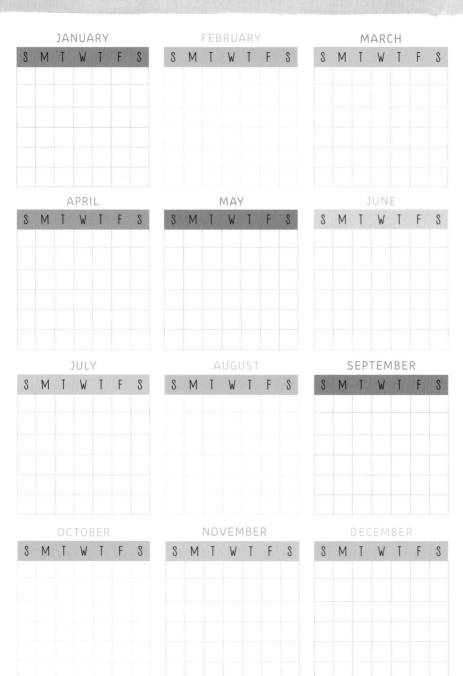

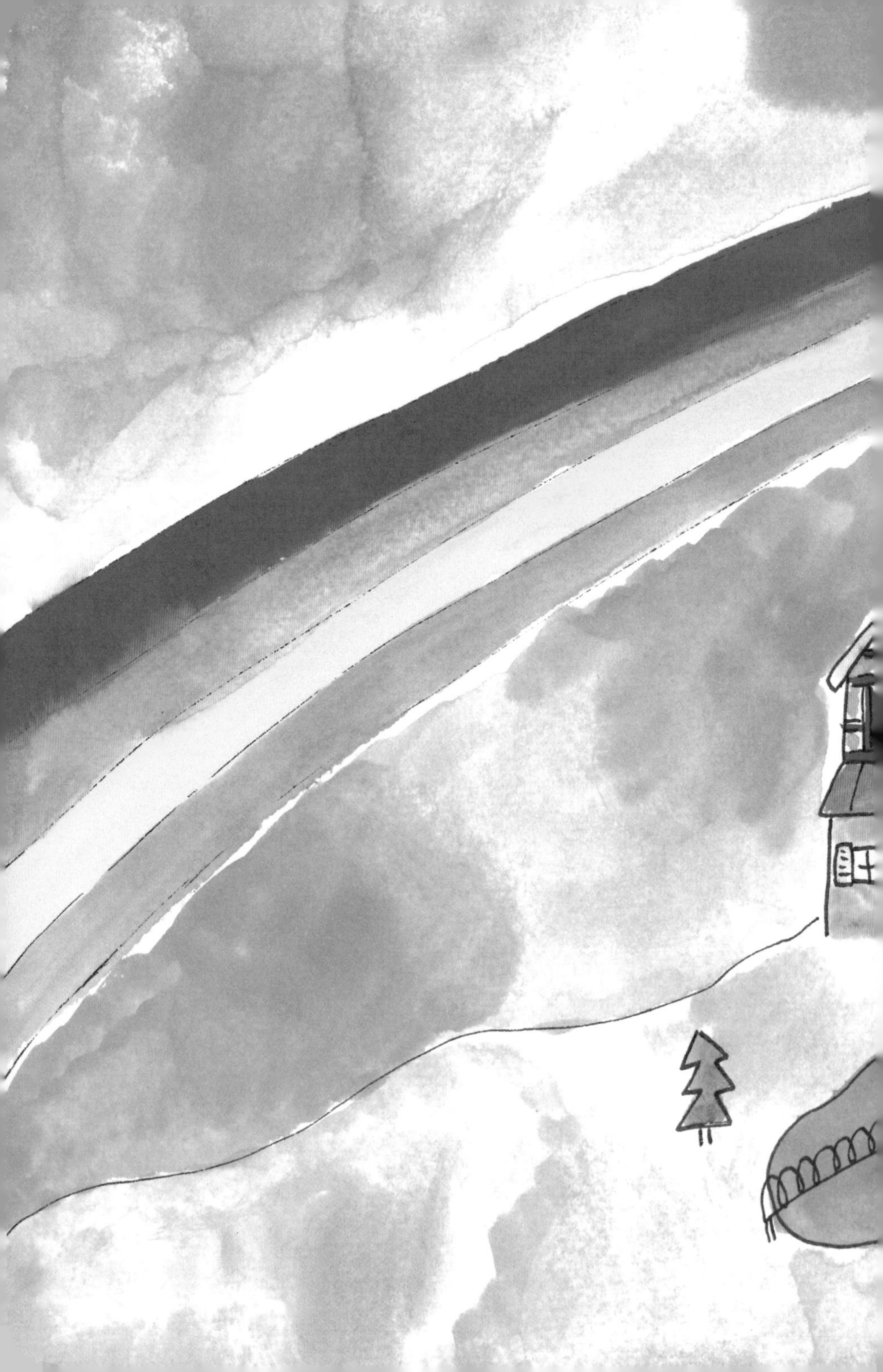

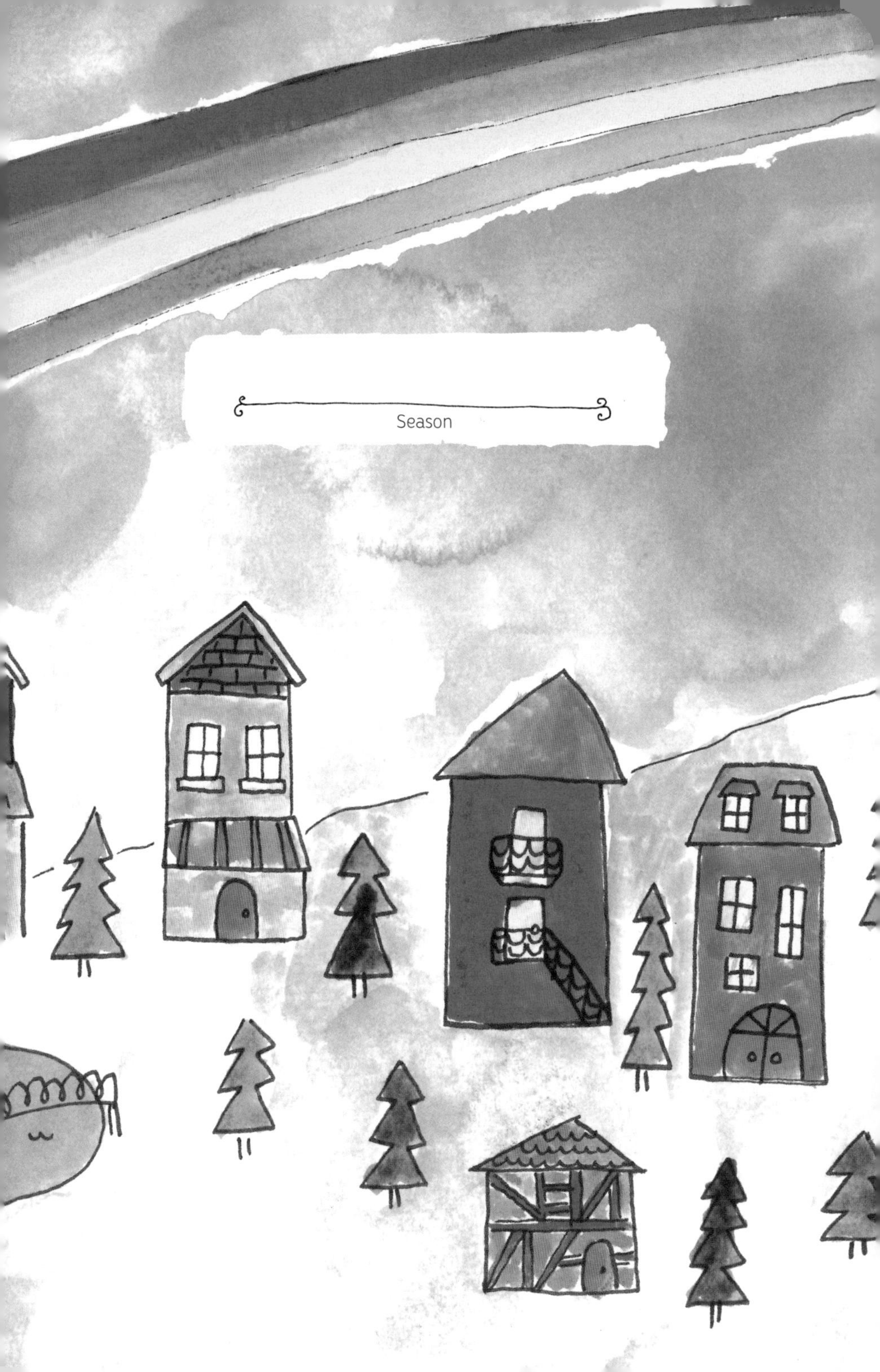
Season

MONTH _____ YEAR _____

MONDAY	TUESDAY	WEDNESDAY	THURSDAY	FRIDAY

MONTHLY
REFLECTION

What are you most proud of right now?

SATURDAY   SUNDAY

PRIORITIES

SPECIAL DATES

MONTH _____ YEAR _____

MONDAY	TUESDAY	WEDNESDAY	THURSDAY	FRIDAY

MONTHLY REFLECTION

What were your wins and losses last month?

SATURDAY   SUNDAY

PRIORITIES

SPECIAL DATES

MONTH _____ YEAR _____

MONDAY	TUESDAY	WEDNESDAY	THURSDAY	FRIDAY

MONTHLY REFLECTION | What do you want to let go of this month?

ATURDAY | SUNDAY

PRIORITIES

SPECIAL DATES

THE SEASON AHEAD

Consider your goals for the three months ahead and find incremental ways to work toward each of your hopes and dreams! You'll get a chance to reflect on how it went after the season is over.

Personal

_____

_____

_____

Work

_____

_____

_____

Wellness

_____

_____

Emotional

_____

_____

Relationships

_____

_____

_____

Family

_____

_____

_____

Special Projects

_____

_____

_____

Other

_____

_____

_____

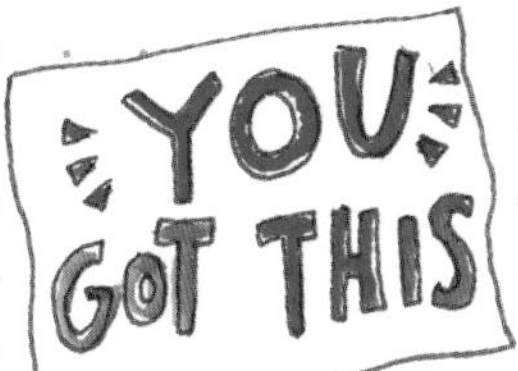
YOU
GOT THIS

Week of: _____

	MONDAY	TUESDAY	WEDNESDAY	THURSDA
6AM				
7				
8				
9				
10				
11				
NOON				
1PM				
2				
3				
4				
5				
6				
7				
8				

Describe your week in one word: What are you grateful for this week?

FRIDAY	SATURDAY	SUNDAY	NOTES

You've felt it before. You'll feel it again.

Habit
Tracker

	M	T	W	T	F	S	S

PLAYBILL

Week of: _____

	MONDAY	TUESDAY	WEDNESDAY	THURSDAY
6AM				
7				
8				
9				
10				
11				
NOON				
1PM				
2				
3				
4				
5				
6				
7				
8				

Describe your week in one word:

What are you grateful for this week?

_____

FRIDAY	SATURDAY	SUNDAY	NOTES

Heartbreak is one of the trade-offs of getting to spend a precious few decades in this world.

Habit
Tracker

	M	T	W	T	F	S	S

Week of: _____

	MONDAY	TUESDAY	WEDNESDAY	THURSDA
6AM				
7				
8				
9				
10				
11				
NOON				
1PM				
2				
3				
4				
5				
6				
7				
8				

Describe your week in one word:

What are you grateful for this week?

_____

FRIDAY	SATURDAY	SUNDAY	NOTES

Habit
Tracker

	M	T	W	T	F	S	S

Never let fear stop you from sending that text, saying it first, trying again, or letting it go.

Week of: _____

	MONDAY	TUESDAY	WEDNESDAY	THURSDA
6AM				
7				
8				
9				
10				
11				
NOON				
1PM				
2				
3				
4				
5				
6				
7				
8				

Describe your week in one word:

What are you grateful for this week?

_____

FRIDAY	SATURDAY	SUNDAY	NOTES

Show up with stories to tell.

Habit
Tracker

M	T	W	T	F	S	S

Week of: _____

	MONDAY	TUESDAY	WEDNESDAY	THURSDA
6AM				
7				
8				
9				
10				
11				
NOON				
1PM				
2				
3				
4				
5				
6				
7				
8				

Describe your week in one word:

What are you grateful for this week?

FRIDAY	SATURDAY	SUNDAY	NOTES

Your small actions will prepare you for the big moments.

Habit
Tracker

M	T	W	T	F	S	S

Week of: _____

	MONDAY	TUESDAY	WEDNESDAY	THURSDA
6AM				
7				
8				
9				
10				
11				
NOON				
1PM				
2				
3				
4				
5				
6				
7				
8				

Describe your week in one word:

What are you grateful for this week?

FRIDAY	SATURDAY	SUNDAY	NOTES

Over time, you will strengthen into a different version of yourself.

Habit Tracker

	M	T	W	T	F	S	S

METRO MAP

Week of: _____

	MONDAY	TUESDAY	WEDNESDAY	THURSDA
6AM				
7				
8				
9				
10				
11				
NOON				
1PM				
2				
3				
4				
5				
6				
7				
8				

Describe your week in one word:

What are you grateful for this week?

FRIDAY	SATURDAY	SUNDAY	NOTES

The colder seasons are the hardest ones to endure, even if you know they won't last forever.

Habit
Tracker

	M	T	W	T	F	S	S

Week of: _____

	MONDAY	TUESDAY	WEDNESDAY	THURSDA
6AM				
7				
8				
9				
10				
11				
NOON				
1PM				
2				
3				
4				
5				
6				
7				
8				

Describe your week in one word: What are you grateful for this week?

FRIDAY	SATURDAY	SUNDAY	NOTES

Habit
Tracker

	M	T	W	T	F	S	S

Now's the time to become the person you want to live with for the rest of your life.

Week of: _____

	MONDAY	TUESDAY	WEDNESDAY	THURSDA
6AM				
7				
8				
9				
10				
11				
NOON				
1PM				
2				
3				
4				
5				
6				
7				
8				

Describe your week in one word:

What are you grateful for this week?

FRIDAY	SATURDAY	SUNDAY	NOTES

Take a step toward joy.

Habit Tracker

M	T	W	T	F	S	S

Week of: _____

	MONDAY	TUESDAY	WEDNESDAY	THURSDA
6AM				
7				
8				
9				
10				
11				
NOON				
1PM				
2				
3				
4				
5				
6				
7				
8				

Describe your week in one word: What are you grateful for this week?

FRIDAY	SATURDAY	SUNDAY	NOTES

Beauty comes in many forms: waves crashing on the rocks or a tiny drop of dew on a peony petal.

Habit Tracker

	M	T	W	T	F	S	S

Week of: _____

	MONDAY	TUESDAY	WEDNESDAY	THURSDA
6AM				
7				
8				
9				
10				
11				
NOON				
1PM				
2				
3				
4				
5				
6				
7				
8				

Describe your week in one word:

What are you grateful for this week?

_____

FRIDAY	SATURDAY	SUNDAY	NOTES

*Kindess =
Niceness +
Wisdom*

Habit
Tracker

	M	T	W	T	F	S	S

Week of: _____

	MONDAY	TUESDAY	WEDNESDAY	THURSDA
6AM				
7				
8				
9				
10				
11				
NOON				
1PM				
2				
3				
4				
5				
6				
7				
8				

Describe your week in one word: What are you grateful for this week?

*Falling in love
with someone
else is a little
bit about falling
in love with
yourself.*

Habit
Tracker

M	T	W	T	F	S	S

Week of: _____

	MONDAY	TUESDAY	WEDNESDAY	THURSDA
6AM				
7				
8				
9				
10				
11				
NOON				
1PM				
2				
3				
4				
5				
6				
7				
8				

Describe your week in one word:

What are you grateful for this week?

FRIDAY	SATURDAY	SUNDAY	NOTES

Fight fate.
Take matters
into your
own hands.
Choose now.

Habit
Tracker

	M	T	W	T	F	S	S

SEASONAL REFLECTION

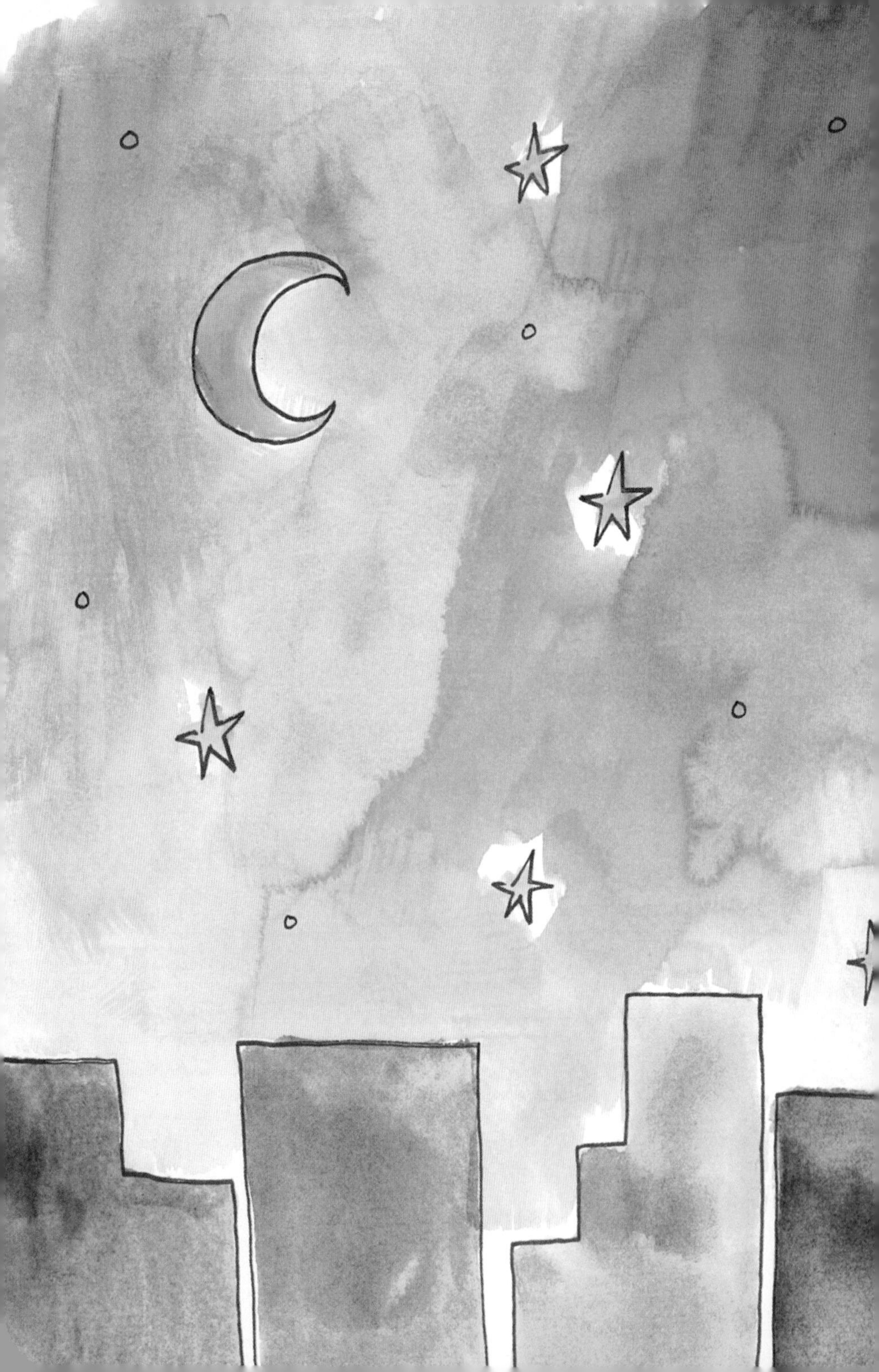

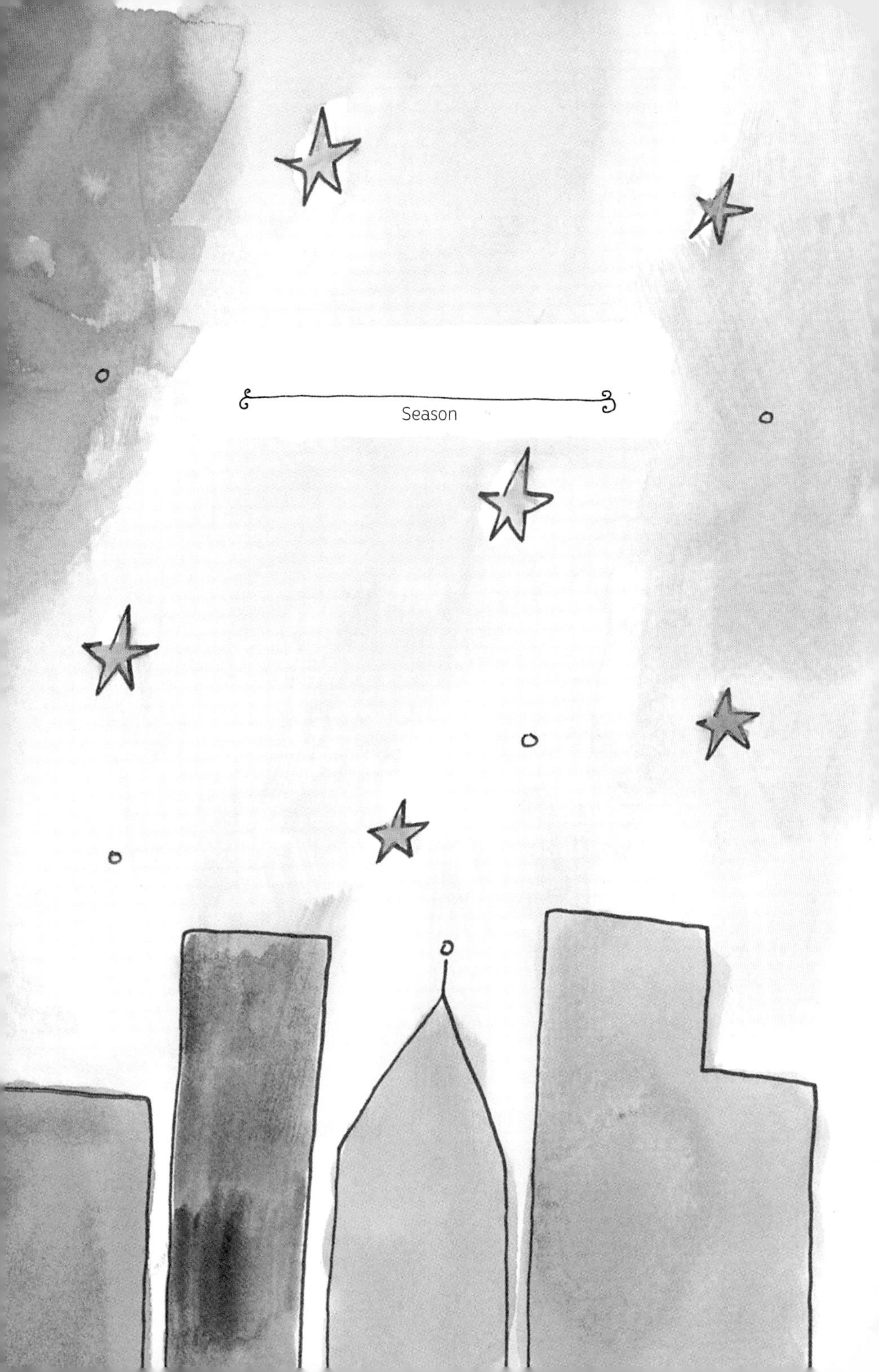
Season

MONTH _____ YEAR _____

MONDAY	TUESDAY	WEDNESDAY	THURSDAY	FRIDAY

MONTHLY REFLECTION

How will you show up for your community this month?

ATURDAY	SUNDAY

PRIORITIES

_____

_____

_____

_____

_____

_____

_____

_____

SPECIAL DATES

_____

_____

_____

_____

MONTH ⸺⸺⸺⸺⸺ YEAR ⸺⸺⸺

MONDAY	TUESDAY	WEDNESDAY	THURSDAY	FRIDAY

MONTHLY
REFLECTION

How will you show up for yourself this month?

SATURDAY | SUNDAY

PRIORITIES

_____

_____

_____

_____

_____

_____

_____

SPECIAL DATES

_____

_____

_____

_____

MONTH &_____& YEAR _____

MONDAY	TUESDAY	WEDNESDAY	THURSDAY	FRIDAY

MONTHLY
REFLECTION

What were your wins and losses last month?

ATURDAY	SUNDAY

PRIORITIES

_____

_____

_____

_____

_____

_____

_____

_____

SPECIAL DATES

_____

_____

_____

_____

THE SEASON AHEAD

Consider your goals for the three months ahead and find incremental ways to work toward each of your hopes and dreams! You'll get a chance to reflect on how it went after the season is over.

Personal	Work
_____	_____
_____	_____
_____	_____

Wellness	Emotional
_____	_____
_____	_____
_____	_____

Relationships	Family
_____	_____
_____	_____
_____	_____

Special Projects	Other
_____	_____
_____	_____
_____	_____

Week of: _____

	MONDAY	TUESDAY	WEDNESDAY	THURSDA
6AM				
7				
8				
9				
10				
11				
NOON				
1PM				
2				
3				
4				
5				
6				
7				
8				

Describe your week in one word:

What are you grateful for this week?

_____

_____

FRIDAY	SATURDAY	SUNDAY	NOTES

Loops, zigzags, stops, and detours won't take you off-course; they push you forward.

Habit
Tracker

M	T	W	T	F	S	S

Week of: _____

	MONDAY	TUESDAY	WEDNESDAY	THURSDA
6AM				
7				
8				
9				
10				
11				
NOON				
1PM				
2				
3				
4				
5				
6				
7				
8				

Describe your week in one word: What are you grateful for this week?

FRIDAY	SATURDAY	SUNDAY	NOTES

To be grateful is a state of attention, not a state of bliss.

Habit
Tracker

	M	T	W	T	F	S	S

Week of: _____

	MONDAY	TUESDAY	WEDNESDAY	THURSDA
6AM				
7				
8				
9				
10				
11				
NOON				
1PM				
2				
3				
4				
5				
6				
7				
8				

Describe your week in one word:

What are you grateful for this week?

_____

FRIDAY	SATURDAY	SUNDAY	NOTES

The people worth impressing: your five-year-old self and your eighty-five-year-old self.

Habit Tracker

	M	T	W	T	F	S	S

Week of: _____

	MONDAY	TUESDAY	WEDNESDAY	THURSDA
6AM				
7				
8				
9				
10				
11				
NOON				
1PM				
2				
3				
4				
5				
6				
7				
8				

Describe your week in one word:

What are you grateful for this week?

_____

FRIDAY	SATURDAY	SUNDAY	NOTES

A new season is a gift; one that gently releases lingering pain and welcomes in new winds.

Habit Tracker

	M	T	W	T	F	S	S

Week of: _____

	MONDAY	TUESDAY	WEDNESDAY	THURSDA
6AM				
7				
8				
9				
10				
11				
NOON				
1PM				
2				
3				
4				
5				
6				
7				
8				

Describe your week in one word:

What are you grateful for this week?

FRIDAY	SATURDAY	SUNDAY	NOTES

It's okay to care about the silly in the midst of the serious, to experience joy in the journey of grief, and to feel disoriented in the meadow of success.

Habit Tracker

	M	T	W	T	F	S	S

Week of: _____

	MONDAY	TUESDAY	WEDNESDAY	THURSDA
6AM				
7				
8				
9				
10				
11				
NOON				
1PM				
2				
3				
4				
5				
6				
7				
8				

Describe your week in one word:

What are you grateful for this week?

FRIDAY	SATURDAY	SUNDAY	NOTES

Habit
Tracker

	M	T	W	T	F	S	S

Create a world in your head and put up a welcome sign.

Week of: _____

	MONDAY	TUESDAY	WEDNESDAY	THURSDA
6AM				
7				
8				
9				
10				
11				
NOON				
1PM				
2				
3				
4				
5				
6				
7				
8				

Describe your week in one word:

What are you grateful for this week?

FRIDAY	SATURDAY	SUNDAY	NOTES

The mind can be the most comforting place to return to at the end of the day.

Habit Tracker

	M	T	W	T	F	S	S

MEX BRASIL

Week of: _____

	MONDAY	TUESDAY	WEDNESDAY	THURSDA
6AM				
7				
8				
9				
10				
11				
NOON				
1PM				
2				
3				
4				
5				
6				
7				
8				

Describe your week in one word: What are you grateful for this week?

FRIDAY	SATURDAY	SUNDAY

NOTES

Progress is slow and gentle.

Habit
Tracker

	M	T	W	T	F	S	S

Week of: _____

	MONDAY	TUESDAY	WEDNESDAY	THURSDA
6AM				
7				
8				
9				
10				
11				
NOON				
1PM				
2				
3				
4				
5				
6				
7				
8				

Describe your week in one word:

What are you grateful for this week?

_____

_____

FRIDAY	SATURDAY	SUNDAY	NOTES

The good doesn't always outweigh the bad, but it usually accompanies the bad, and that companionship can be a source of strength.

Habit Tracker

	M	T	W	T	F	S	S

Week of: _____

	MONDAY	TUESDAY	WEDNESDAY	THURSDAY
6AM				
7				
8				
9				
10				
11				
NOON				
1PM				
2				
3				
4				
5				
6				
7				
8				

Describe your week in one word:

What are you grateful for this week?

FRIDAY	SATURDAY	SUNDAY	NOTES

Optimism takes effort: it's an inward decision with outward action.

Habit Tracker

	M	T	W	T	F	S	S

Week of: _____

	MONDAY	TUESDAY	WEDNESDAY	THURSDA
6AM				
7				
8				
9				
10				
11				
NOON				
1PM				
2				
3				
4				
5				
6				
7				
8				

Describe your week in one word:

What are you grateful for this week?

FRIDAY	SATURDAY	SUNDAY	NOTES

The gift of being in a foreign place is how present it forces you to be; you will notice things in yourself and your surroundings you never knew were there.

Habit
Tracker

	M	T	W	T	F	S	S

Week of: _____

	MONDAY	TUESDAY	WEDNESDAY	THURSDA
6AM				
7				
8				
9				
10				
11				
NOON				
1PM				
2				
3				
4				
5				
6				
7				
8				

Describe your week in one word:

What are you grateful for this week?

FRIDAY	SATURDAY	SUNDAY	NOTES

You don't have to feel optimistic to act from a place of optimism.

Habit Tracker

M	T	W	T	F	S	S

Poetry

Week of: _____

	MONDAY	TUESDAY	WEDNESDAY	THURSDA
6AM				
7				
8				
9				
10				
11				
NOON				
1PM				
2				
3				
4				
5				
6				
7				
8				

Describe your week in one word:

What are you grateful for this week?

FRIDAY	SATURDAY	SUNDAY	NOTES

This world is painful . . . and it is also covered in daffodils.

Habit
Tracker

	M	T	W	T	F	S	S

SEASONAL REFLECTION

MY VALUES

Midyear check-in! What do your values look like these days? Have you learned or prioritized anything new? Take a moment to reflect and jot down your thoughts here.

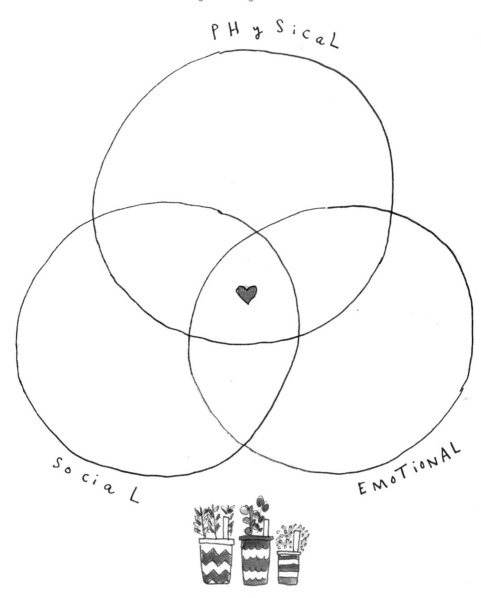

PHySicaL

SociaL

EMoTioNAL

MY VISION BOARD

How's that beginning-of-the-year vision coming along? Time for a refresh!

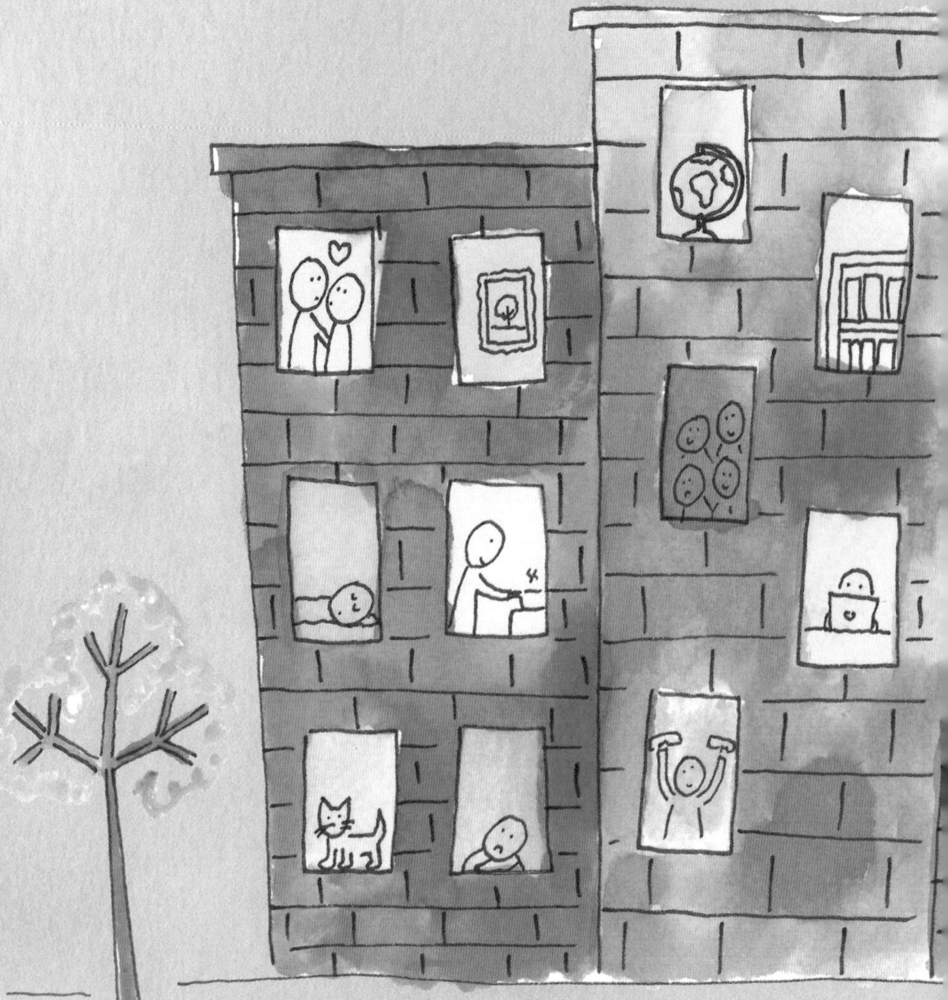

Season

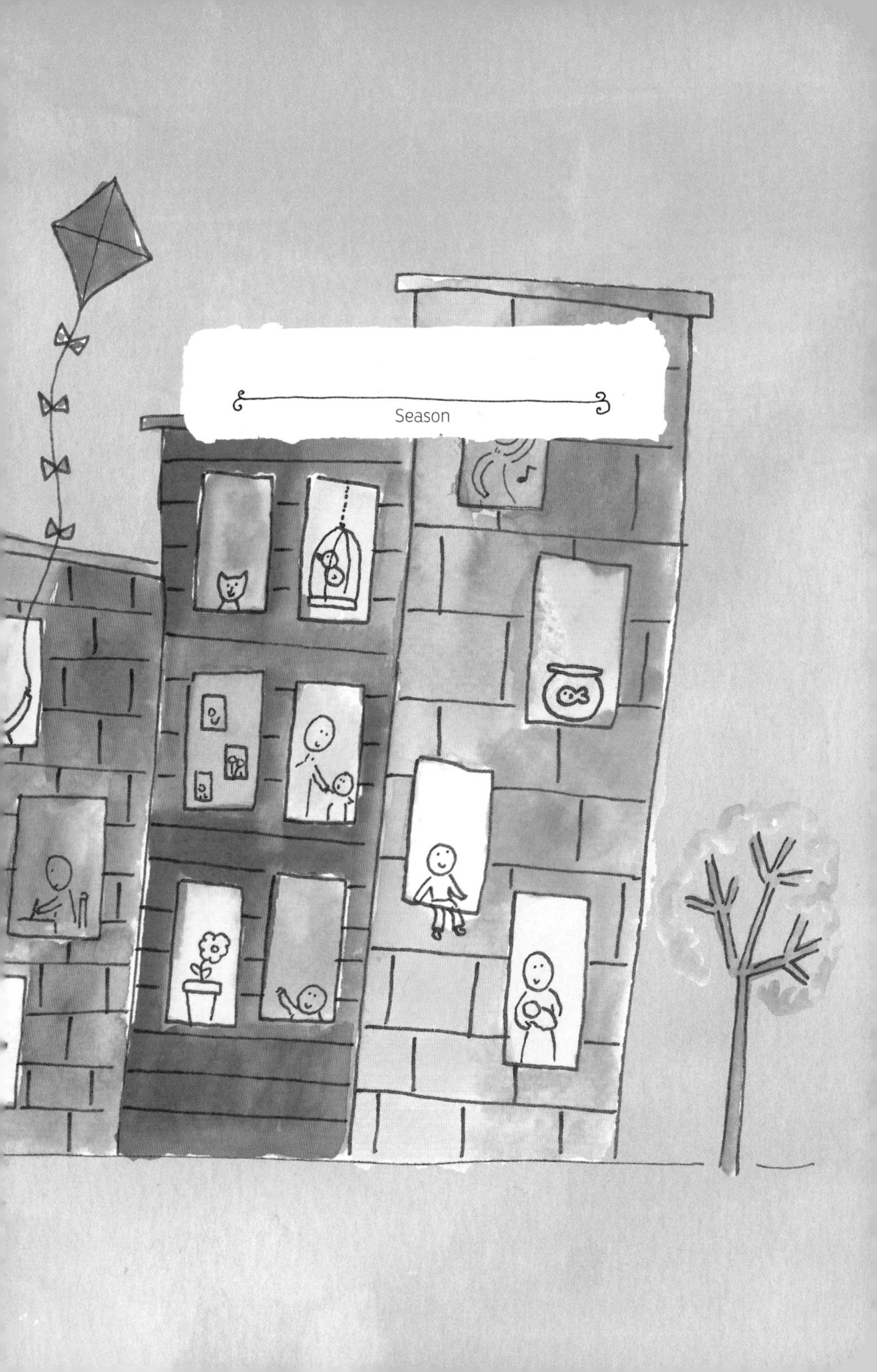

MONTH _____ YEAR _____

MONDAY	TUESDAY	WEDNESDAY	THURSDAY	FRIDAY

MONTHLY
REFLECTION

What are you most proud of right now?

~ATURDAY	SUNDAY

PRIORITIES

_____

_____

_____

_____

_____

_____

_____

_____

_____

SPECIAL DATES

_____

_____

_____

_____

MONTH _____ YEAR _____

MONDAY	TUESDAY	WEDNESDAY	THURSDAY	FRIDAY

MONTHLY REFLECTION | What do you want to let go of this month?

ATURDAY	SUNDAY

PRIORITIES

_____

_____

_____

_____

_____

_____

_____

_____

SPECIAL DATES

_____

_____

_____

_____

MONTH _____ YEAR _____

MONDAY	TUESDAY	WEDNESDAY	THURSDAY	FRIDAY

MONTHLY
REFLECTION

How will you show up for your community this month?

SATURDAY SUNDAY

PRIORITIES

SPECIAL DATES

THE SEASON AHEAD

Consider your goals for the three months ahead and find incremental ways to work toward each of your hopes and dreams! You'll get a chance to reflect on how it went after the season is over.

Personal

_____

_____

_____

Work

_____

_____

_____

Wellness

_____

_____

_____

Emotional

_____

_____

_____

Relationships

_____

_____

_____

Family

_____

_____

_____

Special Projects

_____

_____

_____

Other

_____

_____

_____

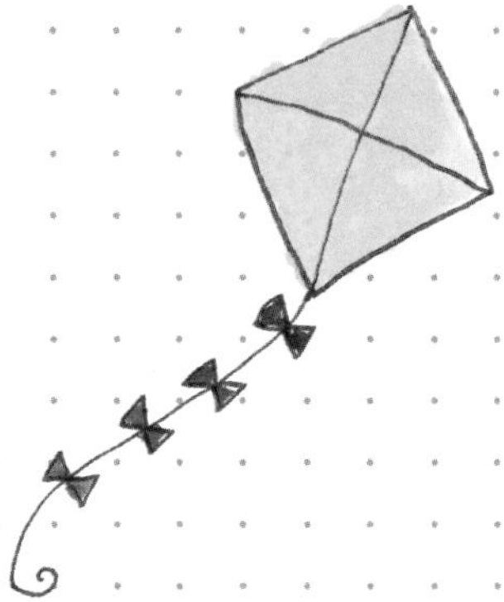

Week of: _____

	MONDAY	TUESDAY	WEDNESDAY	THURSDA
6AM				
7				
8				
9				
10				
11				
NOON				
1PM				
2				
3				
4				
5				
6				
7				
8				

Describe your week in one word:

What are you grateful for this week?

FRIDAY	SATURDAY	SUNDAY	NOTES

Stay flexible with who you think you are.

Habit
Tracker

	M	T	W	T	F	S	S

Week of: _____

	MONDAY	TUESDAY	WEDNESDAY	THURSDA
6AM				
7				
8				
9				
10				
11				
NOON				
1PM				
2				
3				
4				
5				
6				
7				
8				

Describe your week in one word:

What are you grateful for this week?

_____

FRIDAY	SATURDAY	SUNDAY	NOTES

Love =
Curiosity + Time

Habit
Tracker

	M	T	W	T	F	S	S

Week of: _____

	MONDAY	TUESDAY	WEDNESDAY	THURSDA
6AM				
7				
8				
9				
10				
11				
NOON				
1PM				
2				
3				
4				
5				
6				
7				
8				

Describe your week in one word:

What are you grateful for this week?

FRIDAY	SATURDAY	SUNDAY	NOTES

Time is the most precious thing on Earth—it is both magical and fleeting.

Habit
Tracker

	M	T	W	T	F	S	S

Week of: _____

	MONDAY	TUESDAY	WEDNESDAY	THURSDA
6AM				
7				
8				
9				
10				
11				
NOON				
1PM				
2				
3				
4				
5				
6				
7				
8				

Describe your week in one word:

What are you grateful for this week?

FRIDAY	SATURDAY	SUNDAY	NOTES

Don't spend time on people who are not mutually nourishing. Don't do things out of obligation. Don't waste time doubting yourself.

Habit
Tracker

M	T	W	T	F	S	S

Week of: _____

	MONDAY	TUESDAY	WEDNESDAY	THURSDA
6AM				
7				
8				
9				
10				
11				
NOON				
1PM				
2				
3				
4				
5				
6				
7				
8				

Describe your week in one word:

What are you grateful for this week?

_____

FRIDAY	SATURDAY	SUNDAY	NOTES

To strengthen someone does not mean to shout at them "You're strong!" but to whisper "You're scared and I'm with you."

Habit
Tracker

M	T	W	T	F	S	S

Week of: _____

	MONDAY	TUESDAY	WEDNESDAY	THURSDA
6AM				
7				
8				
9				
10				
11				
NOON				
1PM				
2				
3				
4				
5				
6				
7				
8				

Describe your week in one word:

What are you grateful for this week?

FRIDAY	SATURDAY	SUNDAY	NOTES

Make the most of the silence a snowfall brings.

Habit Tracker

	M	T	W	T	F	S	S

Week of: _____

	MONDAY	TUESDAY	WEDNESDAY	THURSDA
6AM				
7				
8				
9				
10				
11				
NOON				
1PM				
2				
3				
4				
5				
6				
7				
8				

Describe your week in one word:

What are you grateful for this week?

FRIDAY	SATURDAY	SUNDAY	NOTES

If you want to get competitive, aspire to be the kindest person.

Habit Tracker

M	T	W	T	F	S	S

Week of: _____

	MONDAY	TUESDAY	WEDNESDAY	THURSDA
6AM				
7				
8				
9				
10				
11				
NOON				
1PM				
2				
3				
4				
5				
6				
7				
8				

Describe your week in one word:

What are you grateful for this week?

FRIDAY	SATURDAY	SUNDAY	NOTES

*Keep working.
That's how
you win!*

Habit
Tracker

	M	T	W	T	F	S	S

WeLCoMe

Week of: _____

	MONDAY	TUESDAY	WEDNESDAY	THURSDA
6AM				
7				
8				
9				
10				
11				
NOON				
1PM				
2				
3				
4				
5				
6				
7				
8				

Describe your week in one word: What are you grateful for this week?

FRIDAY	SATURDAY	SUNDAY	NOTES

*Take cues from
a willow tree:
grounded in
who you are
and free to take
a different shape
with the whims of
the wind.*

Habit
Tracker

	M	T	W	T	F	S	S

Week of: _____

	MONDAY	TUESDAY	WEDNESDAY	THURSDA
6AM				
7				
8				
9				
10				
11				
NOON				
1PM				
2				
3				
4				
5				
6				
7				
8				

Describe your week in one word: What are you grateful for this week?

FRIDAY	SATURDAY	SUNDAY

NOTES

You are writing your own story.

Habit
Tracker

	M	T	W	T	F	S	S

Week of: _____

	MONDAY	TUESDAY	WEDNESDAY	THURSDA
6AM				
7				
8				
9				
10				
11				
NOON				
1PM				
2				
3				
4				
5				
6				
7				
8				

Describe your week in one word:

What are you grateful for this week?

FRIDAY	SATURDAY	SUNDAY	NOTES

True hope has met suffering. True love acknowledges loneliness. True light is informed by darkness.

Habit
Tracker

	M	T	W	T	F	S	S

Week of: _____

	MONDAY	TUESDAY	WEDNESDAY	THURSDA
6AM				
7				
8				
9				
10				
11				
NOON				
1PM				
2				
3				
4				
5				
6				
7				
8				

Describe your week in one word: What are you grateful for this week?

FRIDAY	SATURDAY	SUNDAY	NOTES

You may not always have the same friends or the same relationship you have now, but you'll always be with you.

Habit Tracker

	M	T	W	T	F	S	S

Week of: _____

	MONDAY	TUESDAY	WEDNESDAY	THURSDA
6AM				
7				
8				
9				
10				
11				
NOON				
1PM				
2				
3				
4				
5				
6				
7				
8				

Describe your week in one word:

What are you grateful for this week?

FRIDAY	SATURDAY	SUNDAY	NOTES

Healing doesn't mean you no longer get hurt; it means the hurt doesn't have anything to say about who you are.

Habit
Tracker

	M	T	W	T	F	S	S

YOU GOT THIS

SEASONAL REFLECTION

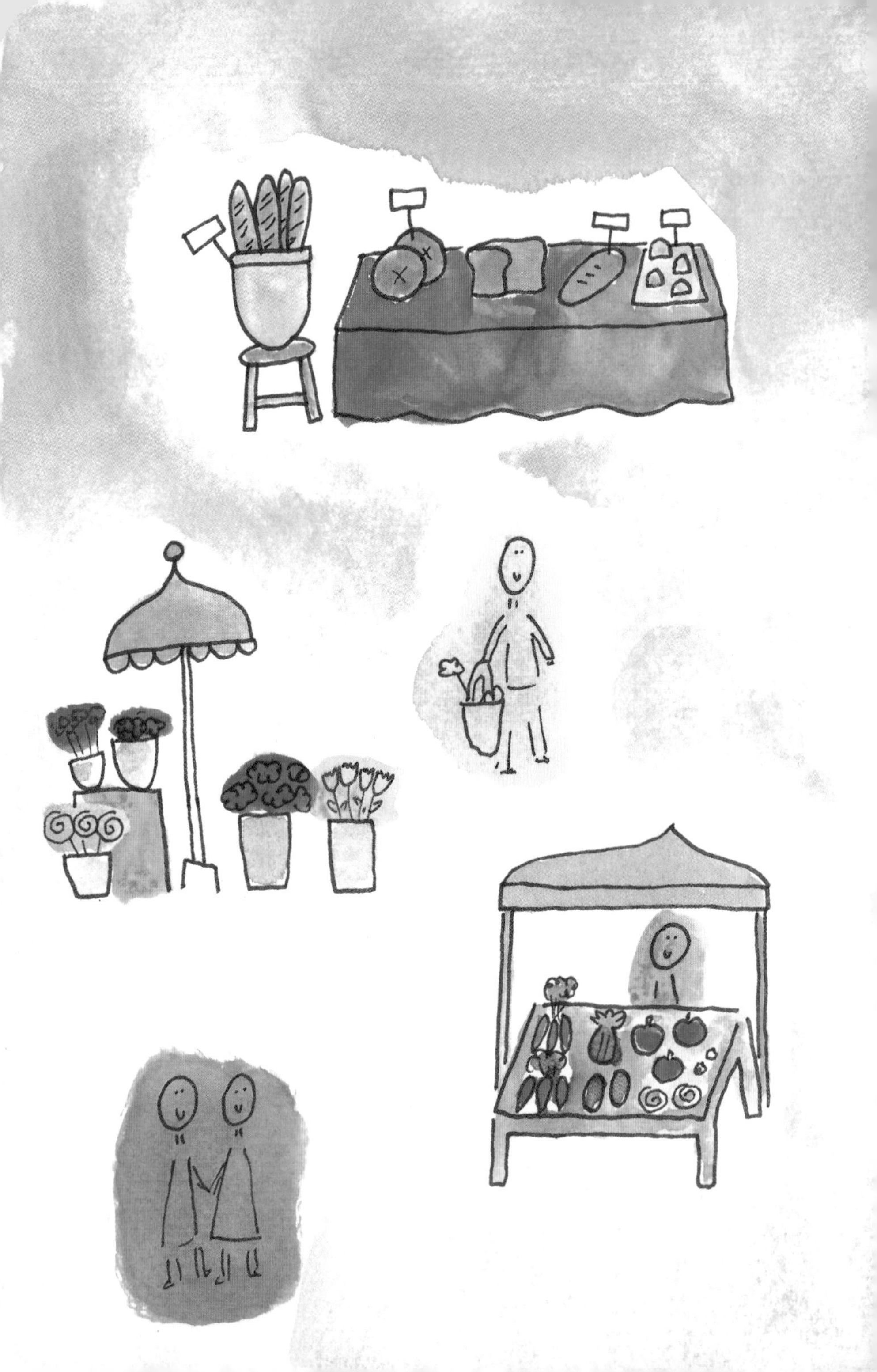

COFFEE

Season

DONUTS

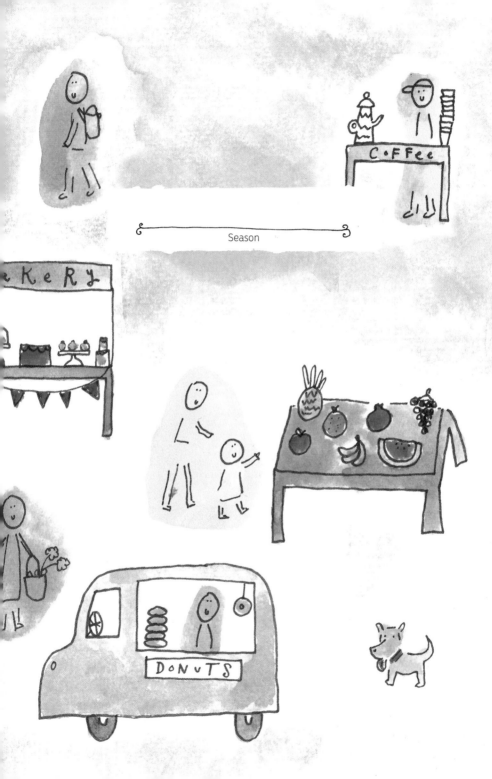

MONTH _____ YEAR _____

MONDAY	TUESDAY	WEDNESDAY	THURSDAY	FRIDAY

MONTHLY REFLECTION

How will you show up for yourself this month?

ATURDAY   SUNDAY

PRIORITIES

_____

_____

_____

_____

_____

_____

_____

_____

SPECIAL DATES

_____

_____

_____

_____

MONTH ⟨_____⟩ YEAR _____

MONDAY	TUESDAY	WEDNESDAY	THURSDAY	FRIDAY

MONTHLY
REFLECTION

What were your wins and losses last month?

ATURDAY	SUNDAY

PRIORITIES

_____

_____

_____

_____

_____

_____

_____

_____

SPECIAL DATES

_____

_____

_____

_____

MONTH _____ YEAR _____

MONDAY	TUESDAY	WEDNESDAY	THURSDAY	FRIDAY

MONTHLY
REFLECTION

What are you most proud of right now?

SATURDAY   SUNDAY

PRIORITIES

_____
_____
_____
_____
_____
_____
_____
_____

SPECIAL DATES

_____
_____
_____
_____

THE SEASON AHEAD

Consider your goals for the three months ahead and find incremental ways to work toward each of your hopes and dreams! You'll get a chance to reflect on how it went after the season is over.

Personal

_____

_____

_____

Work

_____

_____

_____

Wellness

_____

_____

_____

Emotional

_____

_____

_____

Relationships

_____

_____

_____

Family

_____

_____

_____

Special Projects

_____

_____

_____

Other

_____

_____

_____

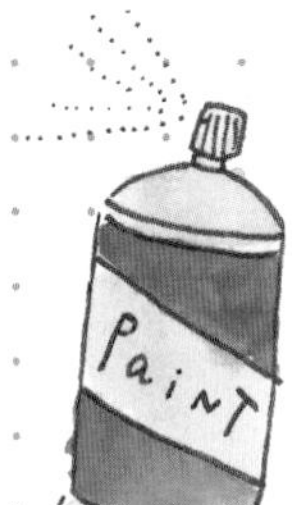
Paint

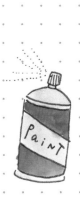

Week of: _____

	MONDAY	TUESDAY	WEDNESDAY	THURSDA
6AM				
7				
8				
9				
10				
11				
NOON				
1PM				
2				
3				
4				
5				
6				
7				
8				

Describe your week in one word: What are you grateful for this week?

_____

FRIDAY	SATURDAY	SUNDAY	NOTES

Boundaries sometimes look more like a flourishing garden than a wall. Pull the weed that doesn't serve you and plant something in its place.

Habit Tracker

M	T	W	T	F	S	S

Week of: _____

	MONDAY	TUESDAY	WEDNESDAY	THURSDA
6AM				
7				
8				
9				
10				
11				
NOON				
1PM				
2				
3				
4				
5				
6				
7				
8				

Describe your week in one word:

What are you grateful for this week?

FRIDAY	SATURDAY	SUNDAY	NOTES

Leave self-consciousness. Take the dance shoes.

Habit Tracker

	M	T	W	T	F	S	S

Week of: _____

	MONDAY	TUESDAY	WEDNESDAY	THURSDA
6AM				
7				
8				
9				
10				
11				
NOON				
1PM				
2				
3				
4				
5				
6				
7				
8				

Describe your week in one word:

What are you grateful for this week?

FRIDAY	SATURDAY	SUNDAY	NOTES

How kind of the world to provide abundant citrus during winter when we are most in need of vitamin C.

Habit tracker

	M	T	W	T	F	S	S

Week of: _____

	MONDAY	TUESDAY	WEDNESDAY	THURSDA
6AM				
7				
8				
9				
10				
11				
NOON				
1PM				
2				
3				
4				
5				
6				
7				
8				

Describe your week in one word:

What are you grateful for this week?

_____

FRIDAY	SATURDAY	SUNDAY	NOTES

Habit Tracker

	M	T	W	T	F	S	S

The brain is flexible.
So is the heart.

Week of: _____

	MONDAY	TUESDAY	WEDNESDAY	THURSDA
6AM				
7				
8				
9				
10				
11				
NOON				
1PM				
2				
3				
4				
5				
6				
7				
8				

Describe your week in one word: What are you grateful for this week?

FRIDAY	SATURDAY	SUNDAY	NOTES

Getting to know yourself doesn't have to be hard work. Marvelous ways to self-reflect: take yourself on a walk, on a date, on an all-night adventure!

Habit Tracker

		M	T	W	T	F	S	S

Week of: _____

	MONDAY	TUESDAY	WEDNESDAY	THURSDA
6AM				
7				
8				
9				
10				
11				
NOON				
1PM				
2				
3				
4				
5				
6				
7				
8				

Describe your week in one word: What are you grateful for this week?

_____

FRIDAY	SATURDAY	SUNDAY

NOTES

Make a city your home by furnishing your mind with mental furniture. Make a person your home by furnishing your heart with emotional furniture.

Habit
Tracker

	M	T	W	T	F	S	S

Week of: _____

	MONDAY	TUESDAY	WEDNESDAY	THURSDA
6AM				
7				
8				
9				
10				
11				
NOON				
1PM				
2				
3				
4				
5				
6				
7				
8				

Describe your week in one word:

What are you grateful for this week?

_____

_____

FRIDAY	SATURDAY	SUNDAY	NOTES

Don't wish for a sky that is only one color.

Habit
Tracker

	M	T	W	T	F	S	S

Week of: _____

	MONDAY	TUESDAY	WEDNESDAY	THURSDA
6AM				
7				
8				
9				
10				
11				
NOON				
1PM				
2				
3				
4				
5				
6				
7				
8				

Describe your week in one word:

What are you grateful for this week?

*Feelings follow
the bread crumbs
of candlelight,
laughter, and
warm voices.*

Habit
Tracker

	M	T	W	T	F	S	S

BEGINNING
ARABIC
مرحبا

Week of: _____

	MONDAY	TUESDAY	WEDNESDAY	THURSDA
6AM				
7				
8				
9				
10				
11				
NOON				
1PM				
2				
3				
4				
5				
6				
7				
8				

Describe your week in one word:

What are you grateful for this week?

FRIDAY	SATURDAY	SUNDAY	NOTES

*Friendship =
Familiarity +
Future*

Habit
Tracker

	M	T	W	T	F	S	S

Week of: _____

	MONDAY	TUESDAY	WEDNESDAY	THURSDA
6AM				
7				
8				
9				
10				
11				
NOON				
1PM				
2				
3				
4				
5				
6				
7				
8				

Describe your week in one word:

What are you grateful for this week?

FRIDAY	SATURDAY	SUNDAY	NOTES

Habit
Tracker

	M	T	W	T	F	S	S

*You don't have
to be an artist to
start making art.*

Week of: _____

	MONDAY	TUESDAY	WEDNESDAY	THURSDA
6AM				
7				
8				
9				
10				
11				
NOON				
1PM				
2				
3				
4				
5				
6				
7				
8				

Describe your week in one word:

What are you grateful for this week?

_____

FRIDAY	SATURDAY	SUNDAY	NOTES

The crack in a heart is an opening for the love of someone who isn't interested in an untarnished past.

Habit
Tracker

	M	T	W	T	F	S	S

Dear FRieND...

Week of: _____

	MONDAY	TUESDAY	WEDNESDAY	THURSDA
6AM				
7				
8				
9				
10				
11				
NOON				
1PM				
2				
3				
4				
5				
6				
7				
8				

Describe your week in one word: What are you grateful for this week?

FRIDAY	SATURDAY	SUNDAY

Take unwanted scraps of life and fertilize growth—be a composter of your soul.

Habit
Tracker

		M	T	W	T	F	S	S

BuBBLe

Week of: _____

	MONDAY	TUESDAY	WEDNESDAY	THURSDA
6AM				
7				
8				
9				
10				
11				
NOON				
1PM				
2				
3				
4				
5				
6				
7				
8				

Describe your week in one word:

What are you grateful for this week?

FRIDAY	SATURDAY	SUNDAY	NOTES

A lot of magic can happen inside your comfort zone.

Habit
Tracker

	M	T	W	T	F	S	S

SEASONAL REFLECTION

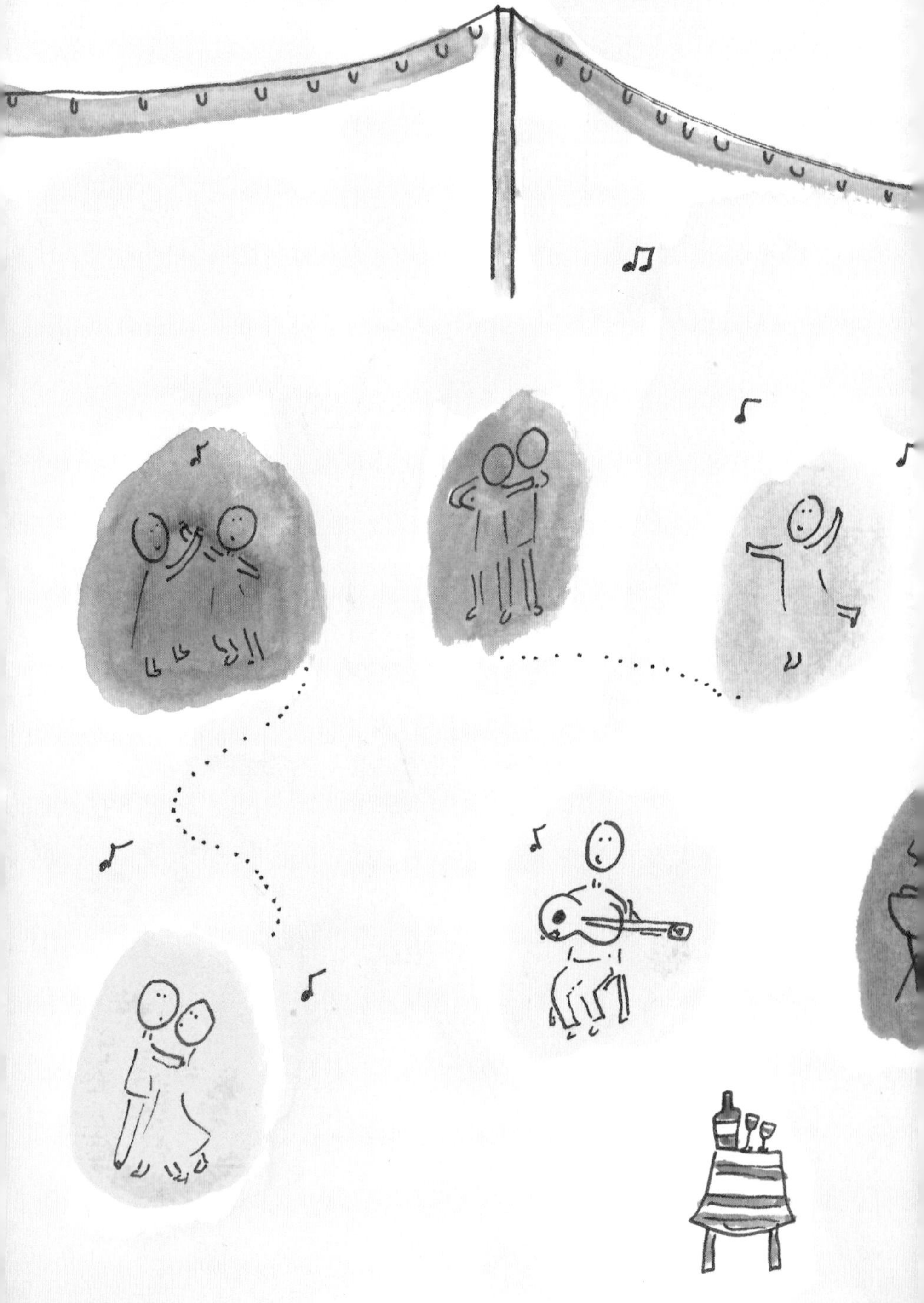

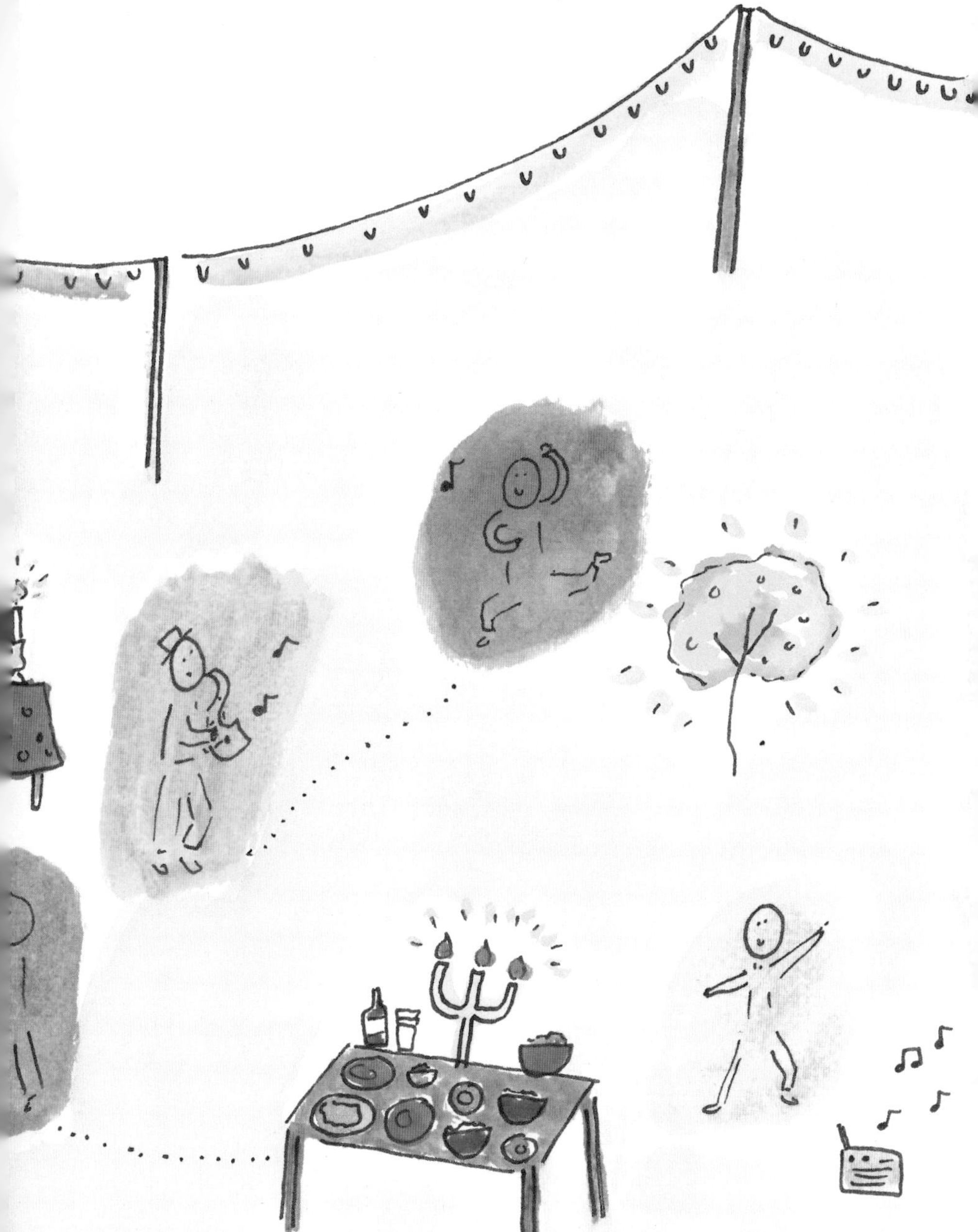

REFLECT ON YOUR YEAR

What did you learn about yourself this year?

_____

_____

_____

How do your friends describe you now? (Feel free to ask!)

_____

_____

_____

How did you get closer to your wildest dreams this year?

_____

_____

_____

Which words or phrases guided you through the year?

_____

_____

_____

Who did you meet this year and who did you get closer to?

_____

_____

_____

How did you feel in your body this year?

_____

_____

_____

What new things did you learn this year?

_____

_____

_____

What progress will you continue to make on your long-term goals?

_____

_____

_____

What are your favorite things about yourself right now?

_____

_____

_____

In what ways did people show up for you this year?

_____

_____

_____

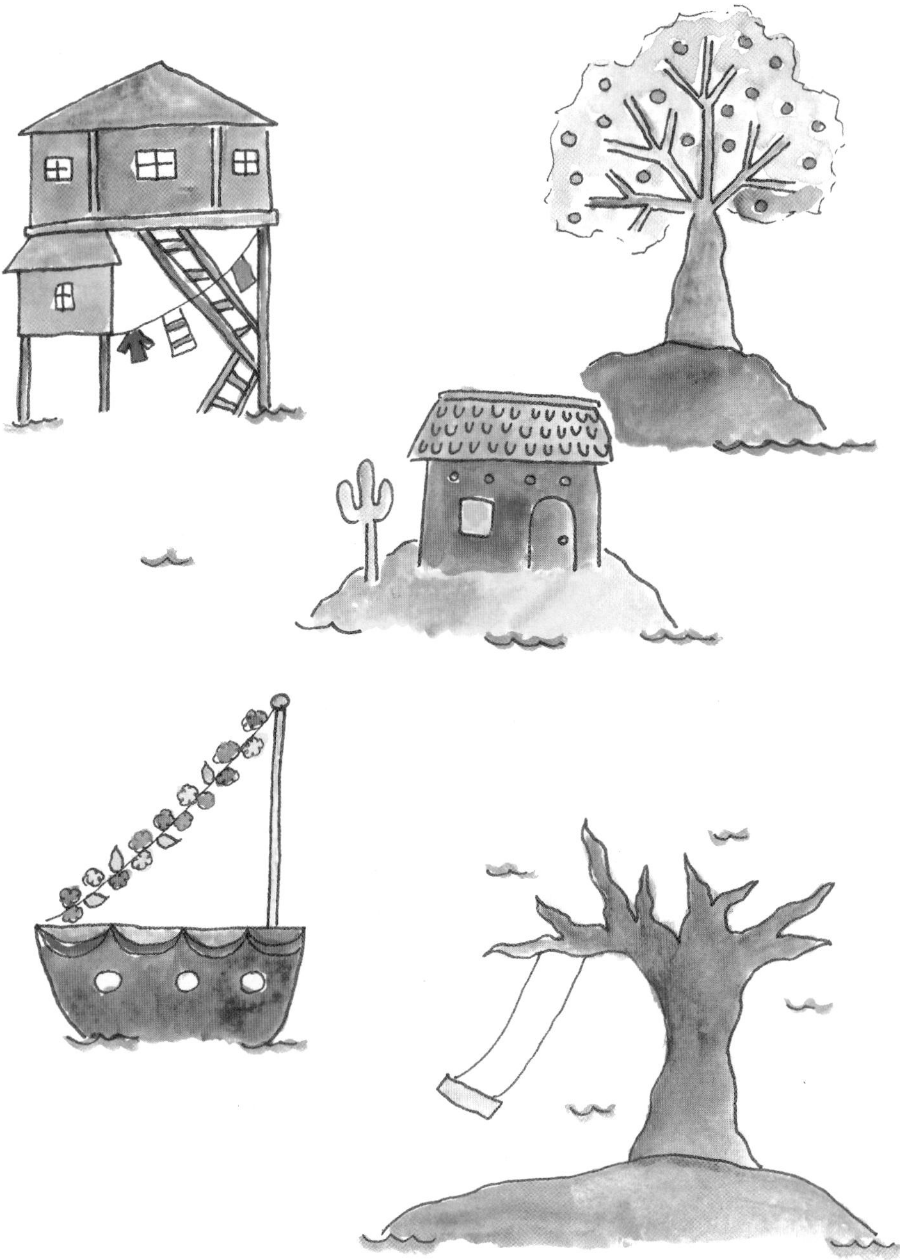

Date Night

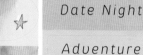

Adventure

ME TIME

Friend time

Friend time

IMPORTANT   DON'T FORGET

NOTE TO SELF   LET'S DO THIS

PRIORITY   REMINDER

Inhale, exhale

Appointment

Appointment

STAY IN

Go outside

ME DAY	TO DO	SICK DAY	DAY OFF
YES I CAN	LET IT GO	HARD DAY	GOOD DAY

Party Time

BILLS DUE

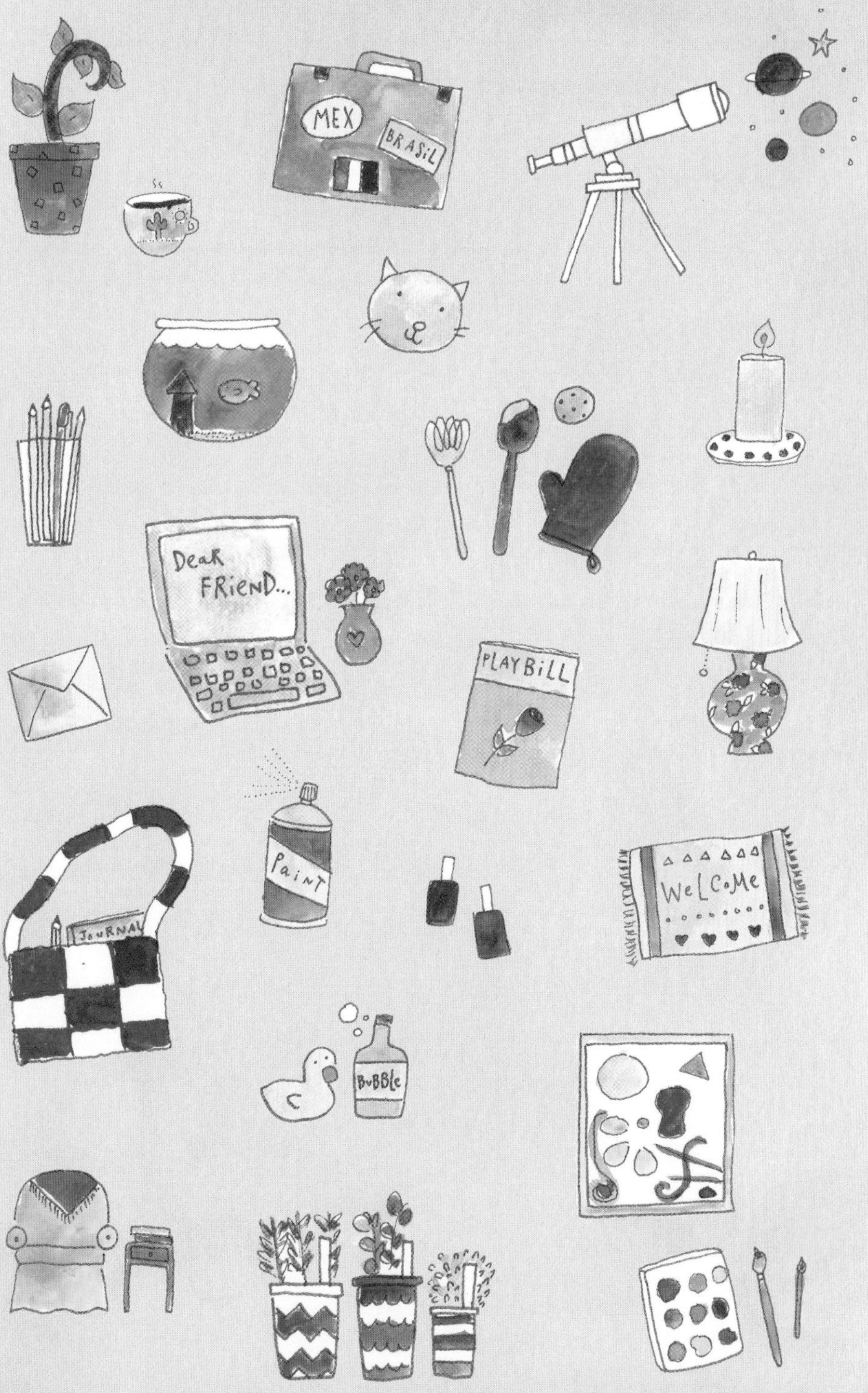
MEX
BRASIL
Dear FRIEND...
PLAYBILL
Paint
WELCOME
BUBBLE

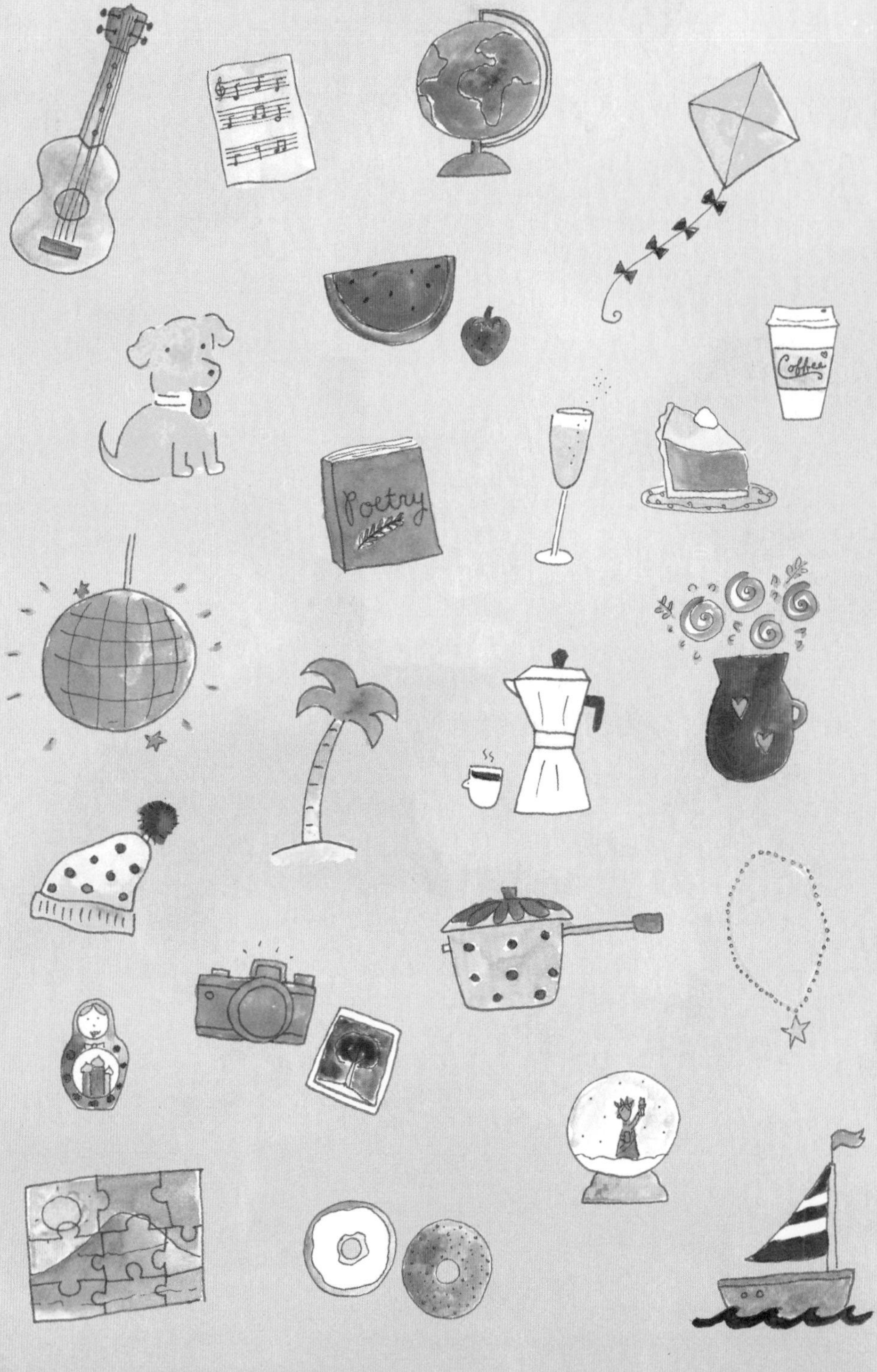
Poetry
Coffee